Waiting for Christmas ....

The stockings were hung ....

JUST FOR YOU!

ockings were hung ....

Waiting for Christmas

COUNTRYMAN

Copyright of illustrations © 2001 by Debra Jordan Bryan
Published by J. Countryman
A division of Thomas Nelson, Inc.,
Nashville, Tennessee 37214

Project Editor—Terri Gibbs

All rights reserved.
No portion of this publication may be
reproduced, stored in a retrieval system or
transmitted in any form by any means—electronic,
mechanical, photocopying, recording, or any other—
except for brief quotations in printed reviews,
without the prior written permission of the publisher.

Designed by Left Coast Design, Portland, Oregon

ISBN: 0-8499-9535-3

www.jcountryman.com

Printed in China

A few
notes of
good cheer
at the
jolliest time
of the
year!

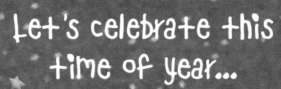

Let's celebrate this
time of year...

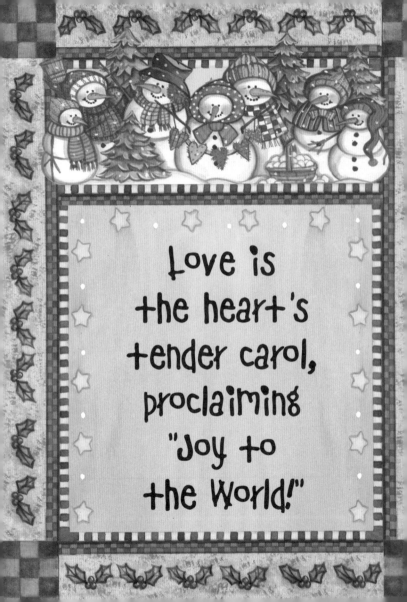

Love is
the heart's
tender carol,
proclaiming
"Joy to
the World!"

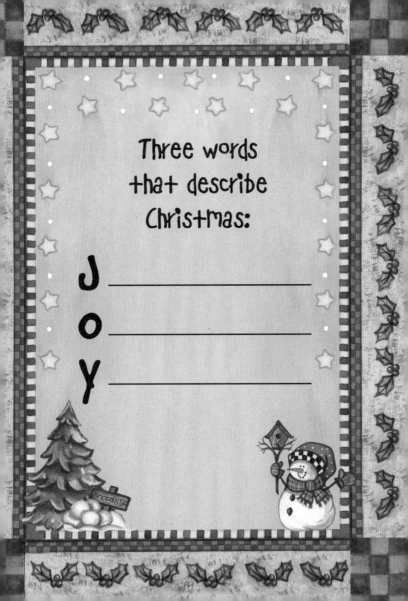

Three words
that describe
Christmas:

J _____

O _____

Y _____

May the glad joy bells of Christmas bring a merry song to your heart!

JOYEUX NOËL

YULETIDE GREETINGS

YULETIDE GREETINGS

JOYEUX NOËL

A gift can
be large,
A gift can
be small,
But a gift
wrapped in love
is the best
gift of all.

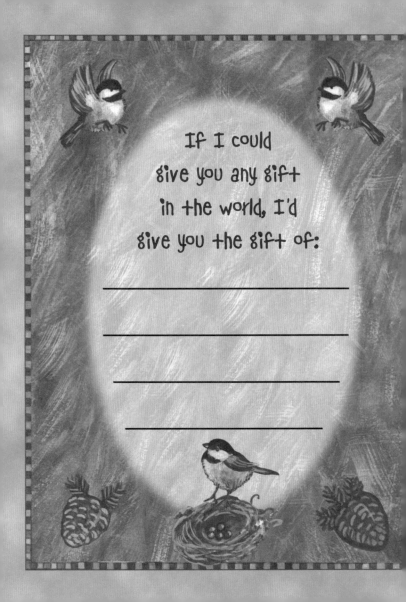

If I could
give you any gift
in the world, I'd
give you the gift of:

_____

_____

_____

_____

TIME FOR GIVING

TIME FOR REMEMBERING

TIME FOR SHARING

TIME FOR LOVING

What sparkles at
Christmas?
Children's eyes, stars
in the sky...

warm hugs and
hearts for others.

Snow and laughter
fill the air,
Christmas joy
is everywhere!

The Stockings were hung ...

A Christmas prayer for you:

_____

_____

_____

_____

_____

_____

_____

_____

Give your Heart

Christmas Blessings

Christmas Blessings

Give your Heart

Keep Friends

close at Christmas

Reindeer food

close at Christmas

Keep Friends

DebraJordanBryan

I hope
you have a
friendly
sort of
Christmas.